THE MINDFUL MILLIONAIRE

Gloria L. Foster

GLOBAL
PUBLISHING
SOLUTIONS

THE MINDFUL MILLIONAIRE by Gloria L. Foster
Published by Global Publishing Solutions, LLC
923 Fieldside Drive
Matteson, Illinois 60443
www.globalpublishingsolutions.com

This book or parts thereof may not be reproduced in any form, stored in a retrieval system, or transmitted in any form by any means—electronic, mechanical, photocopy, recording, or otherwise—without prior permission of the publisher, except as provided by United States of America copyright law.

Copyright © 2024 by Gloria L. Foster

All rights reserved.

International Standard Book Number:
9798330294183
E-book International Standard Book Number:
9798330294190

Unless otherwise indicated, all the names, characters, businesses, places, events, and incidents in this book are either the product of the author's imagination or used in a fictitious manner. Any resemblance to actual persons, living or dead, or actual events is purely coincidental.

Printed in the United States of America

TABLE OF CONTENTS

Introduction - The Evolution of Prosperity i
Foundations of Mindful Prosperity: Exploring Mindful Wealth 1
The Mindful Money Mindset 5
Mindful Investment Strategies 9
The Art of Abundance 21
Mindful Entrepreneurship 25
Mindful Money Habits 29
Mindful Giving and Philanthropy 33
Mindful Wealth and Well-Being 35
Mindful Legacy and Impact 37
Embracing Mindful Prosperity: A Journey of Discovery 41

INTRODUCTION - THE EVOLUTION OF PROSPERITY

In the labyrinth of modern finance and wealth, where success is often measured in numbers and figures, there exists a quieter path—a path illuminated not just by financial gain but by a profound sense of purpose and impact. "The Mindful Millionaire" invites you to embark on a journey beyond traditional notions of wealth, where mindfulness intertwines with prosperity, forging a new paradigm of abundance rooted in holistic well-being and positive influence.

At its core, this book challenges the conventional narrative that equates wealth solely with material accumulation. It posits that true prosperity encompasses a deeper understanding—an awareness that transcends balance sheets to embrace the interconnectedness of personal fulfillment, societal contribution, and environmental stewardship. Here, mindfulness becomes the guiding principle, shaping financial decisions not just for immediate gain but for enduring significance.

Throughout these pages, we explore the multifaceted dimensions of mindful prosperity. We delve into the ways in which mindfulness can enrich not only individual lives but also ripple outwards to enrich communities and ecosystems. Drawing on insights from psychology, economics, and philosophy, we uncover practical strategies and profound philosophies that empower you to cultivate wealth with integrity and purpose.

The journey begins with an exploration of mindfulness itself— not merely as a practice of meditation but as a foundational approach to life and wealth. By cultivating present-moment awareness and clarity of intention, you lay the groundwork for financial decisions that align with your values and aspirations. We delve into mindfulness techniques tailored for wealth-building, from mindful investing and philanthropy to conscious consumerism, illustrating how each choice can resonate far beyond financial gains.

Moreover, "The Mindful Millionaire" champions the role of ethical leadership and governance in shaping a legacy of impact. We examine case studies of visionary leaders who have leveraged their wealth not just for personal gain but for enduring contributions to society—through sustainable business practices, philanthropic initiatives, and advocacy for social justice.

Ultimately, this book is an invitation to reimagine wealth as a force for positive change—a catalyst for fostering compassion, sustainability, and lasting prosperity. Whether you are starting your journey to financial independence or seeking to redefine your existing wealth in more meaningful terms, "The Mindful Millionaire" offers a roadmap to navigate the complexities of wealth with mindfulness and purpose.

Join us as we embark on this transformative odyssey, where the pursuit of wealth aligns seamlessly with the pursuit of well-being and collective flourishing. Together, let us forge a future where mindfulness and prosperity converge to create a world enriched by harmony, abundance, and enduring impact.

FOUNDATIONS OF MINDFUL PROSPERITY: EXPLORING MINDFUL WEALTH

Mindful prosperity begins with a fundamental shift in perspective. It acknowledges that true wealth encompasses more than monetary assets — it includes emotional, spiritual, and social capital. By aligning financial goals with personal values and societal impact, individuals can cultivate a sense of purpose and fulfillment in their pursuit of prosperity.

The roots of mindful prosperity are explored, tracing its philosophical underpinnings through ancient wisdom traditions and modern interpretations. It examines how cultural narratives around wealth have evolved and the emerging trend towards holistic wealth management. Through inspiring stories and insights from thought leaders, readers gain a deeper understanding of the transformative potential of integrating mindfulness into financial decision-making.

Furthermore, the psychological aspects of wealth and well-being are explored, highlighting research on how material wealth alone does not guarantee happiness. It encourages readers to consider their own definitions of prosperity and how these definitions shape their life goals and aspirations. By exploring diverse perspectives on wealth — from minimalism to conscious consumerism — readers are challenged to rethink traditional notions of success and embrace a more balanced approach to personal and societal flourishing.

Practical Exercise: Reflect on your core values and how they influence your financial decisions. Write down three ways you can align your financial goals with these values. Consider how incorporating these values into your financial strategy might lead to greater fulfillment and purpose in your life journey.

THE MINDFUL MONEY MINDSET

A mindful approach to wealth involves cultivating gratitude and intentionality. Gratitude shifts the focus from scarcity to abundance, fostering contentment and attracting positive financial energy. Intentionality ensures that financial decisions are purposeful, reflecting deeper values rather than superficial desires.

This practice of gratitude is explored, with its neuroscientific benefits and its role in rewiring the brain for optimism and resilience. Readers learn practical techniques for incorporating gratitude into their daily lives, from gratitude journaling to mindful appreciation exercises. By fostering a mindset of abundance, individuals are empowered to navigate financial challenges with greater emotional resilience and clarity.

Additionally, the concept of intentionality as a guiding principle in wealth management is explored. It encourages readers to set clear financial goals aligned with their values and aspirations. Through interactive exercises and real-life examples, readers gain practical insights into crafting a financial vision that reflects their deepest intentions and supports their long-term well-being.

Moreover, the common barriers to developing a mindful money mindset are addressed, such as societal pressures and cultural norms. It offers strategies for overcoming these obstacles and cultivating a sense of financial empowerment grounded in personal authenticity and integrity. By reframing financial decision-making through the lens of mindfulness, readers embark on a transformative journey towards a more fulfilling and purpose-driven life.

Practical Exercise: Keep a gratitude journal for a week, noting down three things related to your finances that you're grateful for each day. Reflect on how this practice influences your financial outlook and emotional well-being. Consider how cultivating gratitude can enhance your overall sense of abundance and satisfaction with your current financial circumstances.

MINDFUL INVESTMENT STRATEGIES

Building mindful prosperity extends beyond managing daily finances; it involves making conscious choices in the realm of investments. This investment strategies that align with mindfulness are explored, emphasizing the impact of our financial choices on both personal wealth and the world at large.

Section 1: Understanding Mindful Investing

Mindful investment begins with a shift in perspective — viewing money not just as a tool for personal gain but as a means to create positive change. This section explores the principles of ethical and sustainable investing, highlighting how investors can align their financial goals with environmental, social, and governance (ESG) criteria. By integrating mindfulness into investment decisions, individuals can contribute to a more equitable and sustainable global economy.

The concept of impact investing is explored, where financial decisions are guided by the dual objectives of generating financial returns and achieving measurable social or environmental benefits. Through case studies and real-world examples, readers gain insights into successful impact investors who have leveraged their capital to support causes such as renewable energy, healthcare access, and community development. These stories illustrate the transformative power of mindful investing in addressing pressing societal challenges while generating competitive financial returns.

Furthermore, the section explores the role of diversification in mindful investing, emphasizing the importance of spreading investment capital across different asset classes and geographical regions. By building a diversified portfolio that incorporates sustainable investments, individuals can mitigate risks and capitalize on emerging opportunities in sectors aligned with their values and long-term objectives.

Practical Exercise: Conduct a personal audit of your investment portfolio to assess its alignment with your values and sustainability goals. Identify one investment that you could reallocate towards a more socially responsible or impact-oriented fund. Reflect on how this shift in investment strategy aligns with your broader financial objectives and contributes to positive change in the world.

Section 2: Integrating Mindfulness into Investment Decisions

Mindful investing requires a deep understanding of one's risk tolerance, time horizon, and investment goals. This section guides readers through the process of developing an investment strategy that reflects their values and aspirations. It introduces tools and resources for researching sustainable investment options, from ESG ratings to impact measurement frameworks.

Moreover, the section addresses common misconceptions about sustainable investing, such as the trade-off between financial returns and social impact. It presents evidence that companies with strong ESG practices often outperform their peers over the long term, suggesting that integrating sustainability into investment decisions can enhance portfolio resilience and profitability.

Additionally, the importance of ongoing due diligence and engagement with investment managers and companies is explored. Readers learn how to advocate for transparency and accountability in corporate practices, promoting positive change from within the investment community. By actively participating in shareholder activism and supporting initiatives that align with their values, individuals can amplify their impact and contribute to a more sustainable and equitable global financial system.

Practical Exercise: Choose one company in your investment portfolio and research its ESG performance using publicly available sustainability reports and ratings. Write a letter to the company's investor relations department or board of directors, expressing your support for their sustainability initiatives or raising concerns about areas where you believe they can improve. Reflect on how this engagement enhances your sense of ownership and responsibility as a mindful investor.

Section 3: Building a Sustainable Portfolio

Creating a sustainable investment portfolio begins with identifying investment opportunities that align with personal values and long-term financial goals. This section explores practical strategies for building a diversified portfolio that integrates environmental, social, and governance (ESG) considerations.

Readers are introduced to the concept of thematic investing, where portfolios are structured around specific sustainability themes such as clean energy, water scarcity solutions, or social justice initiatives. By focusing investments on sectors that resonate with their values, individuals can support innovations and businesses driving positive change while potentially benefiting from growth opportunities in emerging markets.

Furthermore, the section delves into the role of financial advisors and investment professionals in guiding sustainable investment decisions. It emphasizes the importance of seeking advisors who are knowledgeable about ESG criteria and can provide tailored recommendations based on individual risk profiles and preferences. By partnering with advisors who share their commitment to mindful investing, readers can access expertise and resources to navigate complex financial markets with confidence.

Moreover, the concept of impact measurement and reporting is explored, highlighting tools and frameworks that investors can use to evaluate the social and environmental outcomes of their investments. By tracking and analyzing impact metrics such as carbon emissions reduction, community engagement, or diversity and inclusion metrics, individuals can assess the effectiveness of their investment strategies in creating positive change.

Practical Exercise: Design a mock sustainable investment portfolio based on your values and sustainability priorities. Research and select at least three companies or funds that align with your chosen sustainability themes. Calculate the potential financial returns and social impact metrics for each investment option. Reflect on how this exercise informs your approach to building a sustainable portfolio that reflects your values and contributes to a more sustainable future.

THE ART OF ABUNDANCE

In the pursuit of mindful prosperity, the mindful millionaire understands that true wealth transcends mere financial accumulation; it encompasses a profound mindset shift from scarcity to abundance. This transformative power of cultivating an abundance mindset is explored, guiding individuals towards a richer and more fulfilling financial existence.

The journey begins with an exploration of the psychology of abundance. Society often conditions us to focus on what we lack rather than appreciating the abundance already present in our lives. Mindfulness practices play a crucial role here, helping individuals recognize and celebrate the wealth that exists in various forms — whether it's health, relationships, opportunities, or personal talents.

Visualization and affirmations emerge as potent tools in shaping an abundance mindset. By envisioning a future abundant with wealth, success, and positive impact, individuals can reprogram their subconscious to attract prosperity. Practical exercises guide readers through visualization techniques and affirmations tailored to their financial goals, reinforcing the belief that abundance is attainable and aligning their actions with this mindset.

Case studies and anecdotes illustrate how individuals have overcome financial challenges by embracing the principles of abundance. By shifting their focus from limitations to possibilities, they've unlocked creative solutions and pathways to financial success. The mindful millionaire understands that opportunities abound for those who cultivate a mindset rooted in positivity and expansive thinking.

Readers are encouraged to practice gratitude as a daily habit. Gratitude not only enhances emotional well-being but also attracts more reasons to be grateful, fostering a cycle of abundance. Practical exercises prompt readers to maintain gratitude journals, reflect on daily blessings, and express appreciation to others, thereby reinforcing their commitment to living abundantly.

Readers grasp that the art of abundance isn't merely about accumulating material wealth; it's about embracing a mindset that celebrates life's richness in all its forms. The mindful millionaire embodies this mindset, recognizing that wealth flows not from scarcity but from a boundless and ever-expanding perspective that enhances both personal fulfillment and financial success.

Practical Exercise: Create a vision board that represents your ideal financial and lifestyle goals. Include images, words, and symbols that resonate with your aspirations for wealth, success, and abundance in all areas of life. Display your vision board in a prominent place where you can see it daily, allowing it to serve as a visual reminder of your intentions and a source of motivation on your journey toward mindful prosperity.

MINDFUL ENTREPRENEURSHIP

Entrepreneurship, approached with mindfulness, becomes a powerful vehicle for both financial success and positive impact. This section explores how the mindful millionaire engages in purpose-driven business practices, creating enterprises that align with values, ethics, and mindful leadership.

Begin by emphasizing the importance of identifying opportunities through a lens of mindfulness. Mindful entrepreneurs keenly observe societal needs and environmental challenges, seeking to create ventures that not only generate profits but also address significant issues. By aligning their businesses with values and purpose, they cultivate enterprises that contribute meaningfully to the world while ensuring sustainable growth.

Mindful leadership takes center stage, highlighting the role of ethics, empathy, and sustainability in business practices. The mindful millionaire understands that ethical decision-making is not just morally imperative but also crucial for long-term success and reputation. Case studies illustrate businesses that have thrived by integrating mindfulness into their organizational culture, fostering environments where employees feel valued, motivated, and aligned with the company's mission.

Innovation becomes a cornerstone of mindful entrepreneurship, driven by conscious creativity and visionary thinking. Entrepreneurs are encouraged to explore how their unique perspectives and ideas can lead to groundbreaking solutions that address pressing societal challenges. Practical guidance is provided on navigating the complexities of business while remaining true to mindful principles, emphasizing the importance of integrity, transparency, and social responsibility.

Throughout this section, readers are invited to envision their entrepreneurial journeys through a mindful lens. They learn how to integrate mindfulness into every stage of business development — from ideation and market research to scaling operations and customer engagement.

By prioritizing purpose alongside profit, they discover that mindful entrepreneurship not only enhances financial success but also creates a positive impact that extends beyond business boundaries.

By the conclusion of this section, readers grasp that mindful entrepreneurship is not merely about launching profitable ventures; it's about leveraging business as a force for good. The mindful millionaire embodies this ethos, recognizing that entrepreneurial success is intertwined with ethical leadership, innovation, and a commitment to making a meaningful difference in the world.

MINDFUL MONEY HABITS

Building mindful prosperity involves not only making mindful financial decisions but also cultivating daily habits that support a balanced and intentional approach to money. The practical aspects of developing mindful money habits are explored, providing readers with actionable steps to enhance their financial well-being.

The journey begins with an exploration of mindful budgeting — an approach that goes beyond restriction and scarcity to focus on aligning spending with personal values. Readers are guided through the process of creating a budget that reflects their priorities, allowing for intentional spending and conscious consumption. Practical exercises highlight the importance of tracking expenses, identifying areas for mindful adjustments, and fostering a healthy relationship with money.

The role of mindfulness in curbing impulsive spending and making intentional financial choices that contribute to long-term financial well-being is emphasized. Savings and emergency funds are examined through a mindful lens, encouraging readers to establish financial safety nets that provide peace of mind and stability. The mindful millionaire understands that financial security is not just about accumulating wealth but also about creating a foundation that withstands unexpected challenges.

Case studies and real-life examples illustrate how individuals have transformed their financial lives by adopting mindful money habits. By prioritizing savings, investing in personal development, and aligning their spending with their values, these individuals have achieved greater financial resilience and freedom. Readers are encouraged to apply these lessons to their own financial journeys, recognizing the transformative power of mindfulness in shaping positive money habits.

Notably, readers will have gained practical tools to incorporate mindfulness into their daily financial routines, fostering a sense of control, contentment, and long-term financial success.

Practical Exercise: Review your current spending habits and identify one area where you can make a mindful adjustment. Create a plan to reallocate those funds towards a savings goal or investment that aligns with your long-term financial objectives. Reflect on how this conscious decision contributes to your overall financial well-being and sense of financial empowerment.

MINDFUL GIVING AND PHILANTHROPY

True wealth extends beyond personal gain; it encompasses the positive impact we make on the lives of others and the world around us. Here, we explore the profound concept of mindful giving and philanthropy, guiding readers on a journey to discover the joy and fulfillment that arises from making a positive difference.

The mindful millionaire recognizes the interconnectedness of humanity and the environment, understanding that their wealth provides an opportunity to contribute to meaningful causes. Here we explore the transformative power of giving, emphasizing that generosity is not only a responsibility but a source of personal fulfillment and purpose.

Readers are introduced to various models of philanthropy, from traditional charitable giving to impact investing and social entrepreneurship. Case studies illuminate the diverse ways in which individuals have leveraged their financial resources to create lasting positive change in areas such as education, healthcare, and environmental conservation. Practical exercises encourage readers to reflect on their values and passions, guiding them to identify causes that resonate with their beliefs.

Here we explore the concept of strategic philanthropy, where financial contributions are aligned with personal values, creating a more significant and lasting impact. Readers will have gained insights into the transformative power of mindful giving. The mindful millionaire understands that wealth, when used mindfully, becomes a force for good — a tool to create positive change, leave a lasting legacy, and contribute to a more compassionate and sustainable world.

MINDFUL WEALTH AND WELL-BEING

The pursuit of mindful prosperity is not solely about accumulating financial wealth; it is about achieving a holistic sense of well-being that extends beyond monetary success. Here we delve into the interconnectedness of wealth and well-being, guiding readers on a journey to nurture both their financial and personal flourishing.

The mind-body connection and its profound impact on overall well-being is explored. Mindful practices, such as meditation and mindfulness exercises, are introduced as tools to enhance mental clarity, reduce stress, and promote a sense of balance in the midst of financial pursuits. The mindful millionaire prioritizes a healthy work-life balance, understanding that sustainable success requires adequate rest, leisure, and time for personal growth.

Practical tips and case studies illustrate how individuals have integrated mindfulness into their daily lives, fostering a sense of fulfillment that extends beyond financial accomplishments. Readers are encouraged to cultivate positive relationships and strong social connections, recognizing the intrinsic value of community and supportive networks.

We explore how mindful wealth-building involves not only personal success but also a commitment to the well-being of those around us. The concept of mindful consumption is introduced, emphasizing the impact of lifestyle choices on both personal health and the environment. Readers are guided to make conscious decisions that align with their values, promoting a sustainable and balanced way of living.

Readers will have gained insights into the symbiotic relationship between wealth and well-being. The mindful millionaire understands that true prosperity is a harmonious integration of financial success, mental and physical health, and positive relationships — a state of being that transcends the limitations of monetary wealth alone.

MINDFUL LEGACY AND IMPACT

In the journey towards mindful prosperity, the concept of legacy emerges as a guiding principle — a testament to the impact we leave on future generations and the world at large. We explore how the mindful millionaire cultivates a legacy that extends beyond financial wealth, shaping a lasting influence rooted in values, ethics, and positive change.

We examine the notion of legacy through a mindful lens, emphasizing that true wealth encompasses more than material possessions. Readers are encouraged to reflect on the imprint they wish to leave on the world, considering how their actions today can resonate far into the future.

Philanthropy as a vehicle for legacy takes center stage, highlighting how mindful giving and strategic investments can create enduring benefits for communities, causes, and institutions. Case studies illustrate how individuals have leveraged their resources to establish foundations, scholarships, and sustainable initiatives that continue to thrive long after their initial contributions.

Environmental stewardship and sustainability become focal points, demonstrating how mindful millionaires prioritize initiatives that promote ecological balance and preserve natural resources for future generations. Readers are inspired to consider how their financial decisions can support environmental conservation efforts and mitigate the impact of climate change.

The importance of ethical leadership and governance in legacy planning, emphasizing transparency, accountability, and a commitment to social responsibility is explored. Readers gain insights into how mindful business practices and ethical frameworks can safeguard their legacy and uphold the values they cherish.

Practical guidance is provided on how to engage family members and heirs in discussions about legacy, ensuring continuity of values and intentions across generations. The mindful millionaire understands that a well-crafted legacy plan not only preserves wealth but also nurtures a culture of stewardship and philanthropy among future beneficiaries.

Here, readers will have gained a comprehensive understanding of how to cultivate a mindful legacy that reflects their values, inspires future generations, and contributes to a world enriched by compassion, sustainability, and enduring prosperity.

EMBRACING MINDFUL PROSPERITY: A JOURNEY OF DISCOVERY

In the culmination of our exploration into mindful prosperity, we find ourselves at the threshold of a profound realization: that true wealth transcends mere accumulation of financial assets. It encompasses a holistic approach to life — a synthesis of mindfulness, purpose, and positive impact.

Throughout this journey, we've delved into the essence of mindful wealth-building, where financial success intertwines with personal values and societal well-being. We've uncovered the transformative power of gratitude, intentionality, and conscious living in shaping a prosperous mindset. From mindful money habits to ethical entrepreneurship, insights into crafting a life of abundance and fulfillment are explored.

At its core, mindful prosperity invites us to redefine wealth not just in terms of monetary riches, but as a reflection of our inner values and contributions to the world. It's about aligning our financial decisions with our deepest aspirations, fostering a sense of harmony and purpose in everything we do.

As we conclude this journey, remember that becoming a mindful millionaire is not an endpoint but a continuous evolution — a commitment to lifelong learning, self-discovery, and mindful living. It's about embracing challenges as opportunities for growth and seeing abundance not as a destination but as a state of being.

May this journey inspire you to cultivate mindfulness in all aspects of your life, to nurture meaningful relationships, and to leave a positive imprint on the world. Let us embark on this ongoing odyssey with open hearts and minds, knowing that each mindful choice brings us closer to a life of true prosperity.

In the words of Lao Tzu, "A journey of a thousand miles begins with a single step."[1] Let your journey towards mindful prosperity begin today.

[1] Quote by Lao Tzu, ancient Chinese philosopher and writer, known for his foundational text, the Tao Te Ching, which emphasizes the principles of Taoism and personal growth.

www.ingramcontent.com/pod-product-compliance
Lightning Source LLC
LaVergne TN
LVHW012049070526
838201LV00082B/3873